I AM NOT AN OLD SOCK

THE RECYCLING PROJECT BOOK

10 AWESOME THINGS TO MAKE WITH SOCKS!

First edition for North America published in 2018
by Barron's Educational Series, Inc.

Text and design copyright © 2018 Carlton Books Limited

Published in 2018 by Carlton Books Limited, an imprint of the
Carlton Publishing Group, 20 Mortimer Street, London W1T 3JW

All inquiries should be addressed to:
Barron's Educational Series, Inc.
250 Wireless Boulevard
Hauppauge, NY 11788
www.barronseduc.com

ISBN: 978-1-4380-1243-8
Library of Congress Control Number: 2018941672

Date of Manufacture: July 2018
Manufactured by: RRD Asia, Kowloon, Hong Kong

Printed in China
9 8 7 6 5 4 3 2 1

Creative Director: Clare Baggaley
Written, designed, illustrated, and
packaged by: Dynamo Limited

The publishers would like to thank the following sources for
their kind permission to reproduce the pictures in this book.
Page 27: Erik Lam/Shutterstock; page 39: Susan Schmitz/Shutterstock
Every effort has been made to acknowledge correctly and contact
the source and/or copyright holder of each picture and Carlton
Books Limited apologizes for any unintentional errors or
omissions that will be corrected in future editions of this book.

I AM NOT AN OLD SOCK

THE RECYCLING PROJECT BOOK

BARRON'S

10 AWESOME THINGS TO MAKE WITH SOCKS!

Hi THERE!

WELCOME TO I AM NOT AN OLD SOCK. It's THE AWESOME BOOK THAT'S PACKED FULL OF EASY-TO-DO CRAFTS AND ARTY PROJECTS FOR THE WHOLE FAMILY.

WE WILL SHOW YOU HOW TO TURN A HUMBLE OLD SOCK INTO A SNOWMAN, COLORFUL OCTOPUS, OR EVEN A SET OF JUGGLING BALLS, PLUS LOTS MORE! IT'S TIME TO GET CREATIVE, SO LET THE FUN BEGIN...

IF YOU PREFER, YOU CAN USE THE HANDY CUTOUTS AT THE BACK OF THE BOOK TO HELP YOU.

YOU'LL NEED A GROWN-UP TO HELP YOU WITH ALL OF THE PROJECTS!

TOP TIP! FABRIC SCISSORS WORK BEST FOR CUTTING YOUR SOCKS BUT PLEASE ALWAYS ASK A GROWN-UP TO DO THIS PART!

YOU WILL NEED

- A VARIETY OF SOCKS IN DIFFERENT COLORS
- GLUE
- TAPE
- SAFETY SCISSORS—FABRIC SCISSORS WORK BEST BUT ALWAYS ASK AN ADULT
- THREAD
- STRING
- BUTTONS
- GOOGLY EYES
- RIBBON
- PENS
- COLORFUL CARDSTOCK OR PAPER
- PIPE CLEANERS
- FEATHERS
- UNCOOKED RICE—FOR FILLING YOUR SOCK CREATIONS
- SCRAPS OF MATERIAL, FABRIC, SOCKS, AND COTTON BATTING FOR STUFFING

CONTENTS

OCTOPUS!

I LIVE IN THE BOTTOM OF **THE OCEAN**, NOT THE BOTTOM OF THE **LAUNDRY BASKET!**

YOU WILL NEED

- 1 COLORFUL SOCK
- STUFFING
- SAFETY SCISSORS
- GLUE
- GOOGLY EYES

LET'S GO FOR A DIP!

SET THE SCENE

Paint blue and green waves onto a piece of oaktag until there is no white remaining, then fill it with cut out fish and exciting sea creatures. You could use tin foil to make super shiny fish and glue on little stones or shells to make a sea floor. Your octopus friends will feel right at home in this watery world.

DID YOU KNOW?

OCTOPUSES HAVE NO BONES BUT THEY DO HAVE 3 HEARTS AND 9 BRAINS!

WITH MY 8 LEGS AND COLORFUL PATTERNS, THERE ARE NO OTHER ANIMALS ON THE PLANET LIKE ME.

GO FURTHER!

FANCY TRYING SOMETHING A LITTLE DIFFERENT? TURN THE PAGE TO MAKE THESE FUNNY FACES.

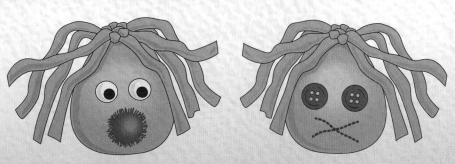

I AM AN OCTOPUS!

1

Push a handful of stuffing to the toe end of your sock to make the body. It should fill up to half-way down your sock.

2

Carefully cut eight strips. Start at the open end of your sock and cut until you have almost reached the stuffing.

3

Hold a leg and tie it in a knot with the leg that is opposite to it. Keep doing this until your octopus stuffing is sealed.

4

Trim the ends of your legs to make points, then glue on some googly eyes.

5

Now you can make lots of octopus pals in different colors!

I AM NOT AN OLD SOCK...

I'M A FABULOUS FUNNY FACE

Have fun making these little guys and gals. Just follow Steps 1–3, then turn your stuffed sock upside down so that the legs become hair. Add some googly or button eyes, then use a button or a small pompom for the nose. Stitch or glue some yarn at the bottom to make a smiley mouth. Who will you create?

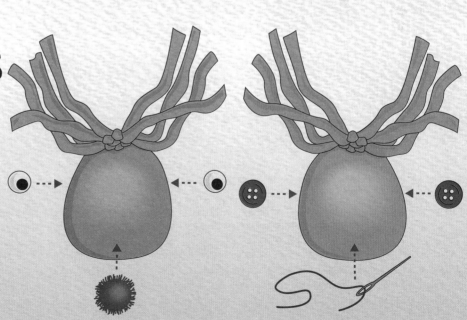

HORSE!

I TROT, CANTER, AND GALLOP. WHY? BECAUSE I AM A HORSE, OF COURSE!

DID YOU KNOW? HORSES CAN SLEEP LYING DOWN OR STANDING UP.

YOU WILL NEED

- 1 SOCK
- CARDSTOCK
- SAFETY SCISSORS
- FABRIC GLUE
- GOOGLY EYES
- YARN
- PINK PAPER
- TAPE

SET THE SCENE

On a large piece of paper, draw a cozy stable for your horse to snuggle up in. Tear up strips of yellow tissue paper to make hay and doodle some apples for it to snack on, too.

LIVING IN THE **COUNTRYSIDE** IS MUCH BETTER THAN ON A **SMELLY OLD FOOT.**

SOMETIMES I EVEN TAKE **PEOPLE** FOR RIDES ALONG THE **BEACH!**

GO FURTHER!

GRAB A STRIPED SOCK AND HEAD OVER TO THE NEXT PAGE TO MAKE A FABULOUS ZEBRA PUPPET.

NEIGHHHHH!

I AM NOT AN OLD SOCK...
I AM A HORSE!

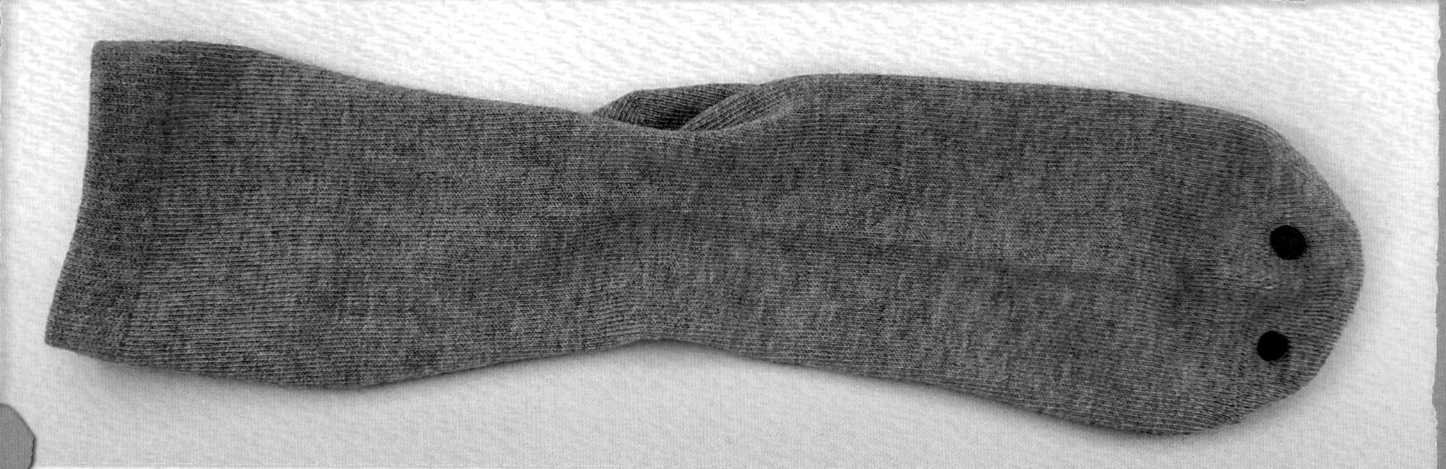

1

Cut two small circles out of cardstock and glue them to the toe part of your sock to make nostrils.

2

Next, glue on some googly eyes.

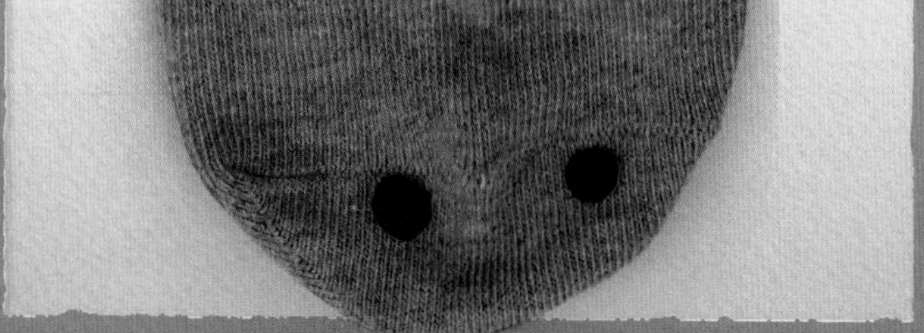

3

Cut two pointy ears out of cardstock, 1½ in (4 cm) long by ¾ in (2 cm) wide. Cut a smaller shape out of pink paper and apply glue to make the inside of each ear.

4 Next, tape or glue your ears onto the sock. You might need to put your hand into the sock to help you see where they need to go.

5 For the mane, cut lengths of yarn and glue them between the ears.

I AM NOT AN OLD SOCK...

I'M A ZEBRA PUPPET!

All you need to make your zebra puppet is a black-and-white striped sock. If you don't have one of those, use fabric paint to paint black stripes onto a plain white sock. Now, simply follow the same steps as the horse puppet! You can add buttons for the nostrils.

JUGGLING BALLS!

WE ARE A **TEAM** OF **JUGGLING BALLS** OFF TO JOIN THE **CIRCUS**!

TOGETHER WE'RE **TONS OF FUN** AND WE JUST **LOVE** BEING CENTER STAGE.

YOU WILL NEED

- 3 SOCKS
- 1 SPOOL OF STICKY TAPE
- 1 HANDFUL OF UNCOOKED RICE

DID YOU KNOW? THE ANCIENT EGYPTIANS USED TO JUGGLE. A PAINTING OF JUGGLING WAS FOUND IN A TOMB!

SET THE SCENE

Make a stage background for your juggling extravaganza. Just hang some fabric or a colorful bedsheet behind you. You could even design your own circus-style sign and make tickets for your show (just make sure you get some practice in, first!).

CAN YOU KEEP US ALL IN THE AIR?

GO FURTHER!

WE WILL SHOW YOU HOW TO MASTER YOUR JUGGLING SKILLS AND IMPRESS ALL YOUR PALS. TURN THE PAGE TO LET THE FUN BEGIN!

I AM NOT AN OLD SOCK...
I'M A SET OF JUGGLING BALLS!

1

Stretch the end of a sock over a spool of sticky tape to keep the sock open. Then, add a handful of uncooked rice.

2

Carefully take the sock off the spool of tape and twist the end of the sock, like this.

3

Next, put your hand into the sock and pull it through completely. It should now look like this:

4

Again, twist the end of the sock, as you did in Step 2. Put your hand into the sock and repeat Step 3.

5

Keep repeating this step until all of the sock material has been used up and you come to the end of your sock.

6

Your finished juggling ball should look like this from the front and the back. Repeat these steps with different colored socks to make a set of 3 juggling balls.

I AM NOT AN OLD SOCK...

NOW LET'S JUGGLE!

Follow this step-by-step guide to teach yourself how to juggle.

1. Start by throwing one sock (ball) high into the air and catching it in your other hand.

2. Now try to throw the ball without looking at it, so that your hand instinctively knows where to go.

3. With one ball in each hand, release one ball to be caught by your opposite hand, then the other.

4. Don't attempt a third ball until you have mastered Step 3! When confident, start with two balls in one hand.

OWL!

TWIT! TWOOO!

I AM A **FEATHERY OWL**, NOT SOME OLD SOCK.

LIVING HIGH UP IN THE TREES I SPEND MY DAYS SNOOZING AWAY...ZZZZ!

AND THEN WHEN NIGHT TIME COMES, I AM **WIDE AWAKE** AND READY FOR **ADVENTURE**.

YOU WILL NEED

- 1 SOCK
- SAFETY SCISSORS
- WADDING (STUFFING)
- FABRIC GLUE
- BUTTONS
- ORANGE PAPER OR CARDSTOCK
- FEATHERS

SET THE SCENE

Make a tree for your owl to perch on by collecting lots of empty cardboard tubes (toilet paper roll, kitchen roll, and wrapping paper tubes work really well!). Paint them brown and tape them together to make a tree shape, adding green tissue paper for leaves.

GO FURTHER!

DID YOU KNOW?
A GROUP OF OWLS IS CALLED A PARLIAMENT.

WHY STOP AT AN OWL? ON THE NEXT PAGE YOU CAN MAKE A SPOOKY BAT.

I AM AN OWL!

1

Lay your sock flat and snip the ankle part away, so that you're left with the foot section. Next, cut this into a pointy shape, so that it looks like the picture, here:

2

Pop a handful of wadding (stuffing) into your sock and fold over both layers of the pointed part, like this, and glue it in place.

3

Glue on two buttons for eyes and a triangle of orange paper to make the beak.

4

Cut some feet out of orange paper.

5

Glue the feet onto the bottom of your owl.

6

Finally glue feathers to each side of your owl to make the wings.

I AM NOT AN OLD SOCK...

I'M A SPOOKY BAT

To make a bat, use a black sock and follow Steps 1 and 2. Add googly eyes and fangs cut out of white cardstock. Cut two red or black feet out of cardstock, and glue to the bottom. Finally, make two flapping bat wings out of black cardstock and glue to each side of your bat's body.

CATERPILLAR!

BEING A CATERPILLAR IS THE GREATEST!

I LOVE TO WRIGGLE UP YOUR GARDEN PATH AND CHOMP ON LEAVES AND FLOWERS THAT I PASS.

BUT BEST OF ALL, ONE DAY I'LL TURN INTO A BUTTERFLY.

CHOMP! CHOMP!

SET THE SCENE

Make a flower bed for your caterpillar to play in. Simply scrunch up small bits of colorful tissue paper into flower shapes and use a dab of glue to stick them onto a green piece of oaktag or cardstock. What will your garden look like?

YOU WILL NEED

- 1 SOCK
- STUFFING
- PIPE CLEANERS
- THREAD
- GOOGLY EYES

GO FURTHER!

ON THE NEXT PAGE, WE WILL SHOW YOU HOW TO MAKE A ROW OF GIANT FLOWERS USING THE SAME TECHNIQUE AS YOUR CATERPILLAR.

CHOMP!

I AM NOT AN OLD SOCK...
I AM A CATERPILLAR!

1

For the caterpillar's face, push a handful of stuffing into the end of the sock. Then twist a pipe cleaner around it to make a ball shape.

2

Repeat Step 1 to make the rest of the sections of your caterpillar's body, until you have a small section of sock left over.

3

When you get to the end of your sock, make the last section the smallest of all and tie with a piece of thread.

4

Use a pipe cleaner to make the antennae. Bend the middle of the pipe cleaner underneath the head to attach it and then curl each end around a pencil to make a coil.

5

Finally, add a red pipe cleaner for a smiley mouth and glue on two googly eyes.

I AM NOT AN OLD SOCK...

I'M A ROW OF FLOWERS

To make a row of flowers from a sock, just follow Steps 1–4, so that you have a long sock that's divided into sections. These will be the base of your flower bed. Next, cut flower shapes out of colorful paper or cardstock and cut out the center of the flower so that you are left with the petals. Now slot the petals over the top of each ball. Use a red pen to draw on specks of pollen.

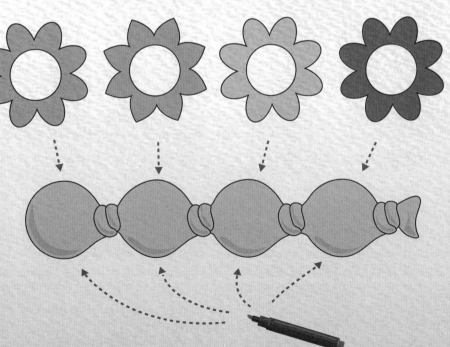

DOG TOY!

I'M A DOG TOY READY TO **PLAY** AND **TUG OF WAR** IS MY **FAVORITE** GAME OF ALL.

LET'S PLAY.

DID YOU KNOW?

DOGS CAN SMELL UP TO 10,000 TIMES BETTER THAN HUMANS CAN.

YOU WILL NEED

- 3 SOCKS IN DIFFERENT COLORS

YOU CAN **GIVE ME** TO **YOUR DOG** AS A **SPECIAL** TREAT WHEN THEY'VE BEEN **EXTRA GOOD.**

WOOF! WOOF!

GO FURTHER!

IF YOU'VE GOT AN EXTRA SOCK, YOU CAN USE THE SAME TECHNIQUE TO MAKE ANOTHER TOY. TURN THE PAGE TO FIND OUT HOW!

I AM NOT AN OLD SOCK...
I AM A DOG TOY!

1 Tie all 3 socks together at the opening by making a knot, as shown.

2 Now, start to braid the socks together by bringing the right sock into the middle, then the left sock into the middle.

3 Keep going until you reach near the bottom, but leave enough space to tie another knot.

4

Finally, tie a knot in this end of your braid to hold it together.

I AM NOT AN OLD SOCK...

I'M ANOTHER DOG TOY!

To make a different type of dog toy, put a dog ball into the end of the sock. Tie a big knot to hold it in place, then cut the leftover sock into 3 strands. Braid these strands and tie another knot in the end and your dog chew is ready! This makes a great toy for playing fetch with, too.

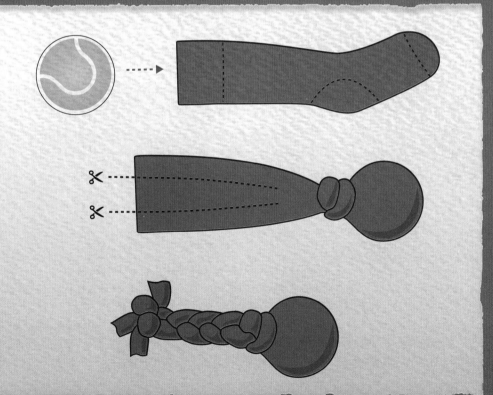

RABBIT!

HOP TO IT...

I **HOP** AROUND ALL OVER THE **GARDEN** AND I **STRETCH UP TALL** TO GET A **GOOD VIEW** OF EVERYTHING.

YOU WILL NEED

- 1 SOCK
- TAPE SPOOL
- UNCOOKED RICE
- YARN OR THREAD
- SAFETY SCISSORS
- COTTON BALL
- GOOGLY EYES
- GLUE
- RIBBON

SET THE SCENE

Cut some tasty veggies out of colorful paper for your bunny to munch on. Try orange carrots, or green cabbages and lettuces. Lay them all out in a cardboard box to create a whole vegetable patch!

HAVE YOU SEEN MY CUTE BOBTAIL AND BIG FLOPPY EARS?

IF YOU BRING ME A CARROT, I'LL BE YOUR FRIEND FOR LIFE.

GO FURTHER!

ONCE YOU'VE MADE ONE RABBIT, WHY NOT USE DIFFERENT-SIZED SOCKS TO MAKE A WHOLE BUNNY FAMILY?

DID YOU KNOW?

WHEN RABBITS ARE HAPPY, THEY JUMP INTO THE AIR AND SPIN AROUND.

I AM NOT AN OLD SOCK...
I AM A RABBIT!

1 Stretch the end of your sock over a spool of tape, like this. This makes it easier to fill your sock with uncooked rice.

2 Fill your sock with uncooked rice until it is roughly ¾ full. Tie up the top of the sock tightly with some yarn or thread.

3 Then use more thread to make a separate head and body shape, like this. Make sure that the rabbit's head is a little bit smaller than the body.

4 To make the ears, cut the ankle part of the sock in half. Then, trim both ends to make them pointy.

5 Make a fluffy bobtail from a cotton ball and glue it to the back of your bunny.

6 Glue on googly eyes and sew a nose and a mouth onto the face. Finish with a sweet ribbon.

I AM NOT AN OLD SOCK...

I'M A WHOLE RABBIT FAMILY

Find different-sized socks to make a whole family of rabbits! Use little socks to make some adorable baby bunnies. What will you name them all?

SNAKE!

I AM NOT AN OLD SOCK, I AM A **SNAKE!**
YOU'LL **KNOW** IT'S ME WITH MY
SCALES AND LONG, **FORKED TONGUE.**

HISSSS!

SET THE SCENE

Shred green tissue paper to make a grassy bank for your snake to hide in.

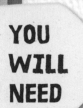

YOU WILL NEED

- 1 SOCK
- STUFFING
- THREAD
- GOOGLY EYES
- RED PIPE CLEANER
- TAPE
- GLUE

GO FURTHER!

IF YOU'RE MORE OF A DOG PERSON, THEN YOU CAN MAKE ONE OF THESE ON THE NEXT PAGE, TOO!

DID YOU KNOW? SNAKES DON'T CHEW THEIR FOOD, THEY SWALLOW IT WHOLE!

I'M THE **CHAMPION** OF **HIDE AND SEEK**, IF WE PLAY IN **LONG GRASS**.

I AM A SNAKE!

1

Begin stuffing your sock with stuffing to make a snake shape.

2

When your sock is stuffed, tie a knot in the end or use thread to keep the stuffing inside.

3

Glue on a pair of googly eyes.

4

Fold a red pipe cleaner in half and twist the ends around each other to make a forked tongue.

5

Tape the tongue onto the front of your snake.

I AM NOT AN OLD SOCK...

I'M A WIENER DOG

Make the body of your dog by using a brown sock for Steps 1–3. Use brown and black cardstock to make ears, a nose, and four legs. Tape them to your wiener dog's body. Finally, make a red tongue out of red felt or cardstock.

CAT TOY!

EXCUSE ME, I AM NOT AN OLD SOCK. I'M A CAT TOY

YOU CAN'T CATCH ME.

YOU WILL NEED

- 1 SOCK
- STUFFING
- SAFETY SCISSORS
- GOOGLY EYES
- GLUE AND TAPE
- STRING

DID YOU KNOW?
CATS SLEEP FOR AROUND 16 HOURS EVERY DAY!'

BEING **SUPER PLAYFUL** MEANS THAT I CAN KEEP **KITTIES** ON THEIR **TOES**— I MEAN **PAWS!**

GO FURTHER!

KEEP YOUR KITTY REALLY INTERESTED IN THEIR NEW TOY WITH OUR TOP TIPS ON THE NEXT PAGE.

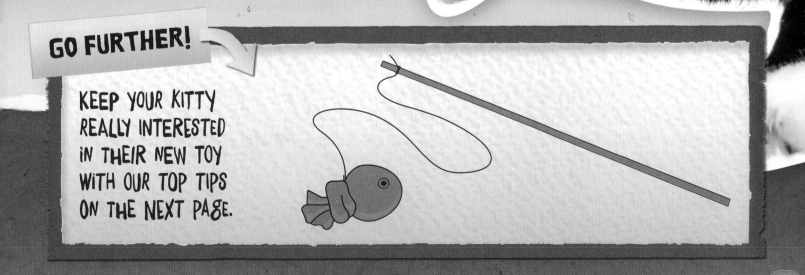

I AM NOT AN OLD SOCK...
I AM A CAT TOY!

1 Push a little ball of stuffing into the end of a sock.

2 Now tie a knot in the sock to keep the stuffing in place.

3 Cut the end of the sock off and neaten up the edges.

4 You could add a googly eye to make your toy look more like a fish.

5

Next, tape or sew your cat toy to a piece of string and you're ready to play!

I AM NOT AN OLD SOCK...

TOP TIPS!

To make your cat toy even better, tie it to a stick and wiggle it around so your cat chases after it. You could even put catnip or a treat inside the sock to make your cat really interested!

SNOWMAN!

BEING FROSTY AND ICY COLD IS MY FAVORITE WAY TO BE, BECAUSE I AM A SNOWMAN!

DID YOU KNOW?
JAPAN IS THE SNOWIEST PLACE IN THE WORLD.

BRRRR!

BRRRR!

YOU WILL NEED

- 1 WHITE SOCK
- STUFFING
- 1 COLORFUL SOCK
- THREAD
- BUTTONS
- BLACK PEN
- ORANGE PAPER
- GLUE
- SAFETY SCISSORS

I LOVE TO DRESS UP IN A BIG COZY HAT AND SCARF. JUST CHECK OUT MY COAL EYES AND CARROT STICK NOSE!

SET THE SCENE

Make a frosty background scene for your snowman to stand in. Use cotton balls for snow and bits of tin foil for slippery ice. Glue them onto a piece of blue cardstock. Try drawing more snowmen in the picture to keep your snow sock buddy company!

I'M THE SNOWMAN THAT NEVER MELTS!

GO FURTHER!

LET'S MAKE A SOCK PENGUIN TO ADD TO YOUR SNOWY SCENE, TOO. WE WILL SHOW YOU HOW ON THE NEXT PAGE.

I AM NOT AN OLD SOCK...
I AM A SNOWMAN!

1 Push stuffing into a white sock. Leave enough space so that you can tie a knot in the end.

2 Trim around the knot to neaten it up. Now, make a scarf from a strip of colorful sock and tie it around the white sock to make a head and body.

3 Take the rest of the colorful sock and cut the ankle part off like this. Pinch it into a hat shape and tie some thread around it to keep it in place.

4 Put the hat on the snowman's head. Now it's time to glue some brightly colored buttons onto the snowman's tummy.

5

Draw on two eyes and a smile using a black pen.

6

Cut a carrot nose out of orange paper and glue it onto your snowman's face.

I AM NOT AN OLD SOCK...

I'M A PENGUIN

Stuff a black sock so that it's around ¾ full and tie a knot in the top. Next, tie a piece of thread around the penguin to make a head and body shape. Cut out round pieces of white fabric (you could use a piece of a white sock) and glue them on to make the penguin's tummy and face. Add googly eyes, tape on a yellow paper beak, and make a hat and scarf from a colorful sock.

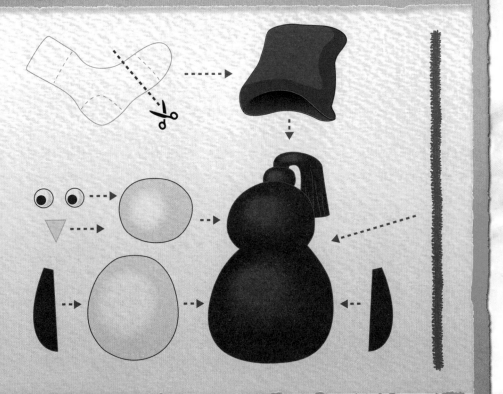

YOUR DESiGNS

NOW iT'S YOUR TURN... THE ONLY THiNG HOLDiNG YOUR OLD SOCKS BACK FROM GREATNESS iS YOUR OWN iMAGiNATiON! SKETCH YOU iDEAS HERE—WE'VE GiVEN YOU A COUPLE OF OUTLiNES TO GET YOU STARTED.

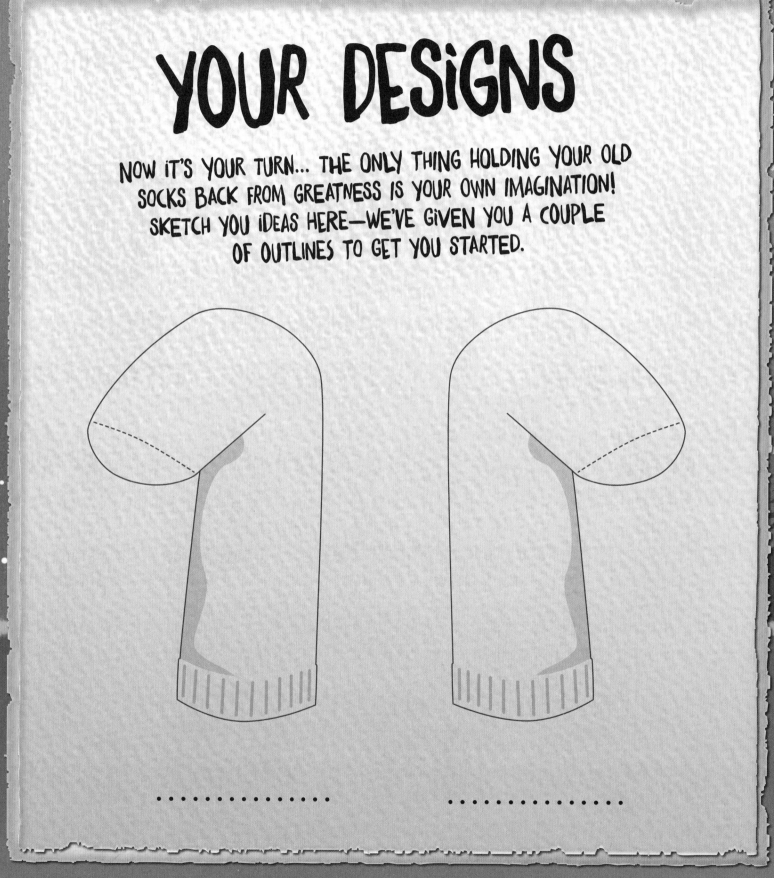

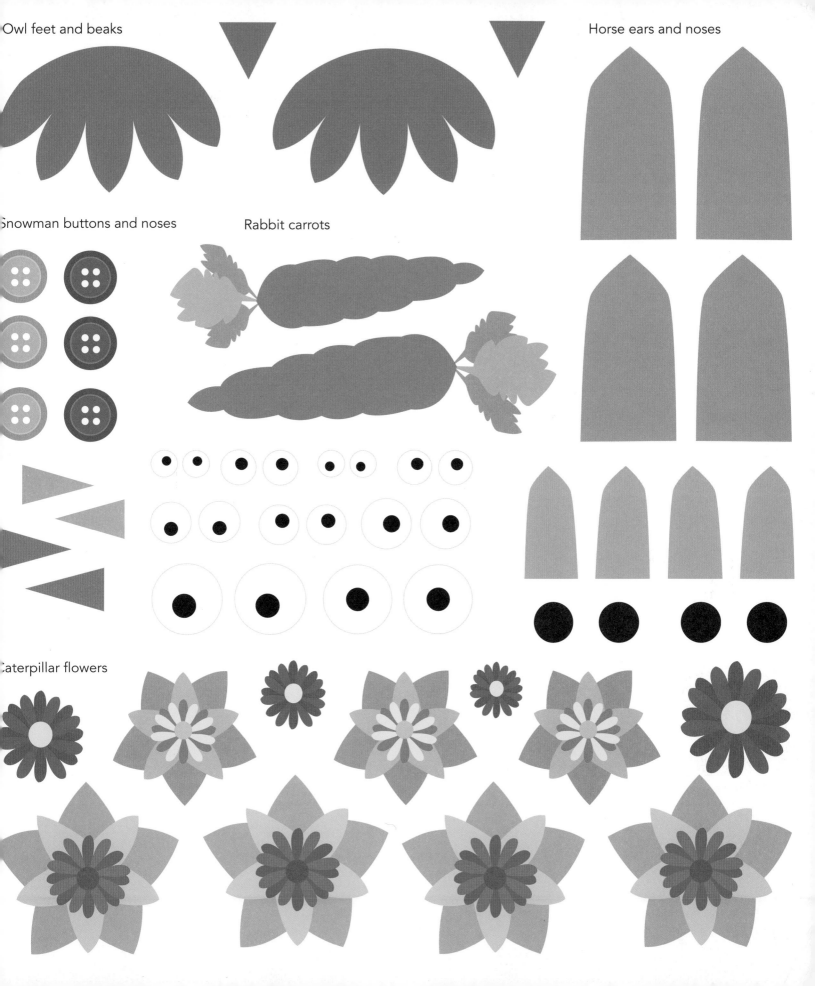

Owl feet and beaks

Horse ears and noses

Snowman buttons and noses

Rabbit carrots

Caterpillar flowers